Enthusiast's Complete Restaurant Guide

Andrew Delaplaine

Andrew Delaplaine is the Food Enthusiast.
When he's not playing tennis, he dines anonymously
at the Publisher's (considerable) expense.

Senior Editors — Renee & Sophie Delaplaine
Senior Writer — James Cubby
Art Director — Charles McGoldrick

Gramercy Park Press
New York – London – Paris

Please submit corrections, additions or comments to
gppress@gmail.com

SEATTLE

The Food Enthusiast's
Complete Restaurant Guide

Table of Contents

INTRODUCTION

A trip to the Pacific Northwest is not complete with a stop in Seattle. Seattle is a distinctive city and is recognized for many reasons. Some know Seattle as the setting for Seattle Grace, the hospital of the television series "Grey's Anatomy," while others think of Seattle as the home of grunge, a type of music popular in the early 1990s. Almost everyone associates Seattle with the **Space Needle**, the city's most recognizable landmark erected for the 1962 Century 21 Exposition. Seattle is filled with coffee shops, cafes and has even been labeled "the city of coffee." After all, this is the site of the very first Starbucks store.

Seattle, the largest city in the Pacific Northwest, is known for many things and happens to be one of the fastest growing cities in the U.S. The Seattle metropolitan area is the biggest in the U.S. Seattle is also a major seaport, and is a major gateway for trade with Asia.

Seattle is a thriving city welcoming visitors year round. There is much to do and see in Seattle from its walkable Downtown where you'll find the famous **Pike Place Market**, the oldest farmers' market in the United States, and the location of the original Starbucks, which is still in operation, to the **Pioneer Square - Skid Road Historic District** marked by the triangular plaza and the unique architecture with several buildings listed on the National Register of Historic Places.

Seattle is a beautiful city with spectacular views like the spectacle of the two incredible mountain rages on either side of Puget Sound, the snow-capped Olympics and the Cascades. **Mount Rainier**, the tallest volcanic peak of the Cascade Range, rises above the city. The picturesque Elliot Bay acts as a looking glass for one of the world's most stunning city skylines. Speaking of views, a visit to Seattle is not complete without a stop at the **Space Needle** that is as high as a 60-story building and affords visitors a 360-degree view of the city, mountains and sea.

Seattle is a popular arts and culture destination, second only to New York is presenting new theatre works. Visitors and residents can enjoy an impressive year-round schedule of performances from the likes of the **Seattle Symphony Orchestra**, the **Seattle Opera**, the **Pacific Northwest Ballet**, and the **Seattle Youth Symphony** Orchestras, the largest symphonic youth organization in the United States. The **Seattle Chamber Music Society** presents annual chamber music festivals during the summer and winter. Seattle boasts approximately 100 theatrical companies performing in over two dozen theatre venues. One such venue, the 5th Avenue Theatre, offers Broadway-style musical shows featuring international stars.

Seattle's thriving music scene attracts music lovers filling both small venues and large arenas. While Seattle is a melting pot for a variety of musical types it will always be known as the "home of grunge" because artists like Nirvana, Soundgarden, Alice in Chains, and Pearl Jam, called Seattle home. The jazz scene continues to thrive and the city is home to a variety of well-known artists like avant-garde jazz musicians Bill Frisell and Wane Horvitz. Culture lovers should not miss a visit to the **EMP Museum** (formerly the Experience Music Project and **Science Fiction Museum and Hall of Fame**) that hosts a variety of programs including an annual battle-of-the bands, the **Science Fiction and Fantasy Short Film Festival**, **Pop Conference** -- an annual gathering of music critics, musicians and fans, and showcases rare artifacts from pop music history.

Seattle has a wonderful selection of museums and cultural resources. **Seattle Art Museum** (SAM), located near the downtown central corridor, exhibits a diverse collection of modern and classical art. The **Henry Art Gallery**, part of the University of Washington, located in the University District, is known for its exhibitions of cutting-edge contemporary art. The **Burke Museum of Natural History and Culture** features a variety of exhibitions including Northwest Coast Indian art and artifacts. The **Bellevue Arts Museum** (BAM) shows modern and contemporary exhibitions of craft arts. The **Museum of History and Industry** (MOHAI) shares the history of Seattle in a variety of exhibitions and programs. The **Seattle Asian Art Museum**, an affiliate of SAM, features exhibitions of Asian art and is located in the Capitol Hill neighborhood.

Dining in Seattle is an adventure and visitors are often overwhelmed with so many excellent restaurants. Wine connoisseurs rate Washington state wines among the best in the world. There are many boutique wineries in the Seattle area, including the celebrated **Chateau Ste. Michelle** (15 miles from Seattle). The truly adventurous will want to tour the wineries in Seattle and some of the neighboring towns like Woodinville, Leavenworth, Wenatchee, Chelan, Yakima, or Walla Walla and discover Seattle's increasingly important boutique wine industry.

GETTING ABOUT

I will say that Seattle has one of the most confusing grid systems for its streets (for newcomers especially) than any I've seen anywhere. Even in ancient cities where they had no grid at all—Rome, London, Paris—getting around seems much easier. In New York, planners didn't even begin applying a grid-like scheme for the city until the 19th Century. I still get momentarily confused when I'm below Canal Street. Anywhere above 14th Street is easy as it can be.

Not like here in Seattle.

Here's why:

The roads that run North-South are called "avenues" while roads that run East-West are called "streets." Of course, unless you have a compass with you, how can you tell which ways is East and which way is North?

To complicate matters even more, the city is separated into seven directional sections: SW, NW, NE, N, S, W, E.

It gets worse:

The addresses for the **STREETS** are labeled with the section *in front of* the street number, so an address would read like this: NE 23rd Street. Locals will just say NE 23rd, because they know if the NE is in front of the street number that it's a street and not an avenue.

The addresses for the **AVENUES**, however, are labeled with the section *after* the avenue. Thus, 23rd Avenue NE. Or, as a local would put it, 23rd NE.

In Downtown, the streets are actually named, such as Jefferson, Columbia, Madison, etc.

You must be absolutely sure when giving an address to a bus driver or cabbie. Don't get more confused than you are already.

The public transit system here, **METRO TRANSIT**, is the best way to get around if you don't have a car.

http://metro.kingcounty.gov

They have an effective **Trip Planner** service that works pretty well:

http://tripplanner.kingcounty.gov

Fares are only a couple of dollars, but you have to have exact change, as drivers don't handle any cash.

RapidRide

Red and yellow buses serve these special routes. These buses show up every 10 minutes.

http://metro.kingcounty.gov/travel-options/bus/rapidride

Seattle Streetcar

It's not a Streetcar Named Desire, but it's very effective, and is expanding. Runs from Downtown along the South Lake Union Line.

www.seattlestreetcar.org

Seattle Center Monorail

www.seattlemonorail.com

This line connects Downtown and the Seattle Center (where you'll find the famous Space Needle).

Bikes

A lot of people use bikes, but the streets are usually damp from all the drizzle, so you have to be careful.

The address issue is only a problem if you've never been to Seattle before. Once you spend a week here, you'll get the hang of it. And you can ask most anybody. The people are extremely outgoing and friendly, as if they live in their own little world.

Which of course, they do, because Seattle is unlike any other place you'll ever visit.

The A to Z Listings

Ridiculously Extravagant
Sensible Alternatives
Quality Bargain Spots

ALTSTADT BIERHALLE & BRATHAUS
209 First Ave. S, Seattle, 206-602-6442
www.altstadtseattle.com/
CUISINE: German
DRINKS: Full Bar
SERVING: Lunch & Dinner
PRICE RANGE: $$
NEIGHBORHOOD: Pioneer Square
This place is indeed inspired by beer halls of Germany with a menu of reinvented German classics. Menu favorites include standards like Bratwurst, pork, veal, beef, duck and pretzels. Great selection of unique beers and liquors. Flat screen TVs for sports fans.

ANALOG COFFEE
235 Summit Ave. E, Seattle, No Phone
www.analogcoffee.com
CUISINE: Coffee
DRINKS: No Booze

SERVING: Breakfast, Lunch & Late Afternoon
PRICE RANGE: $
Small neighborhood coffeehouse with beer on tap.
Here you'll also find a nice selection of muffins and
breakfast snacks. They were the first people in town
to offer "cold brew on tap," and you'll find this coffee
really smooth and highly concentrated. You'll find
loads of comic books and records. (They'll even
exchange coffee for your records.)

ALTURA
617 Broadway (bet. Mercer & Roy), Seattle, 206-402-6749
alturarestaurant.com/
CUISINE: Italian
DRINKS: Full bar; reasonable wine list
SERVING: dinner Tuesday-Sunday from 5:30; closed Monday
PRICE RANGE: $$$$
NEIGHBORHOOD: Capitol Hill
Plush service is a hallmark of this romantic candlelit spot with
mellow music in the background. In a town where "come as you
are" is sometimes taken to extremes (all those dressed-down
software engineers from Microsoft and Amazon), Altura offers
something much nicer than the average. Chef Lockwood serves
up variously priced 3 or 5-course menus, with or without wine
pairings. (He has a cavatelli accented with a duck liver sauce. Or
go for the pappardelle with braised tripe and oxtail ragu. Tripe
normally makes me want to barf, but not here. The scallops
wrapped in pancetta will have you rolling your eyes.

ASSAGGIO RESTAURANTE

2010 Fourth Ave, Seattle, 206-441-1399

www.assaggioseattle.com

CUISINE: Italian

DRINKS: Full bar

SERVING: Mon – Fri lunch and dinner, Sat dinner only, closed Sun

PRICE RANGE: $$$

NEIGHBORHOOD: Belltown

Located in the heart of downtown, this comfortable 100-seat restaurant offers unpretentious Italian fare in an upscale atmosphere. Menu favorites include: Carpaccio and the Pettini di Mare (seared sea scallops with wild mix greens).

THE ATHENIAN
Pike Place Market

1517 Pike Pl, Seattle, 206-624-7166

www.athenianinn.com

CUISINE: Seafood/American

DRINKS: Full Bar

SERVING: Breakfast, Lunch & Dinner

PRICE RANGE: $$

NEIGHBORHOOD: Downtown

Known as one of the locations for the film "Sleepless in Seattle." Low-key eatery with a simple menu featuring breakfast, seafood, burgers, and other hearty fare like salmon and chips. There's a seafood lasagna that's pretty damn tasty, too. It's been in business since 1909.

BA BAR
550 12th Ave, Seattle, 206-328-2030
www.babarseattle.com
CUISINE: Vietnamese
DRINKS: Full bar
SERVING: Daily breakfast, lunch, and dinner
PRICE RANGE: $$
NEIGHBORHOOD: Central District
This intimate little restaurant offers a menu of tasty Vietnamese street food. Menu favorites include: Duck Noodle and Combo Vermicelli.

BAGUETTE BOX
1203 Pine St, Seattle, 206-332-0220
www.baguetteboxseattle.com
CUISINE: Asian Fusion/Sandwiches
DRINKS: Beer & Wine
SERVING: Lunch, and dinner
PRICE RANGE: $
NEIGHBORHOOD: Capitol Hill
This gourmet sandwich shop specializes in Vietnamese-style

sandwiches and other Asian fare, but the owner here has lately expanded his offerings to embrace big deli-style sandwiches stuffed into his ever so tasty crusty baguettes. Menu items include: baguettes, paninis, rice bowls, and salads. The also offer lunch boxes to go.

BALLARD PIZZA COMPANY
5107 Ballard Ave NW, Seattle, 206-946-9960
www.ballardpizzacompany.com
CUISINE: Pizza, Italian
DRINKS: Beer & Wine
SERVING: Lunch, and dinner
PRICE RANGE: $$
NEIGHBORHOOD: Ballard
This pizzeria offers a great menu serving whole pies and "fat slices." Menu favorites include: Arugula Salad and Veggie Pizza. Delivery and pick up options.

BLUEACRE SEAFOOD
1700 Seventh Ave, Seattle, 206-659-0737
www.blueacreseafood.com
CUISINE: Seafood, Live/Raw Food
DRINKS: Full bar
SERVING: Daily lunch and dinner
PRICE RANGE: $$$
NEIGHBORHOOD: Denny Triangle
This seafood restaurant features a menu of fresh wild seafood as well as farmed freshwater oysters, clams, and mussels. The bar offers a nice selection of cocktails, wines and craft beers. Menu favorites include: Cappy's Spicy Cioppino (a seafood stew with gulf shrimp, fin fish and shellfish) and Olive Crusted Alaskan Halibut.

BRAVE HORSE TAVERN

310 Terry Ave N, Seattle, 206-971-0717

www.bravehorsetavern.com

CUISINE: American

DRINKS: Full bar

SERVING: Lunch, and dinner

PRICE RANGE: $$

NEIGHBORHOOD: South Lake Union

This friendly tavern (over 21 only) offers a comfortable option for dinner or a late-night snack with a menu of burgers, sandwiches, and salads. Bar offers over 36 types of beer on tap and games like shuffleboard and darts. This is a favorite for Sunday Brunch.

THE BROOKLYN

1212 2nd Ave, Seattle (b/t Seneca St & University St), 206-224-7000

www.thebrooklyn.com

CUISINE: Seafood/Steakhouse/Live Raw Food

DRINKS: Full bar

SERVING: Lunch/Dinner; Dinner only on Sat & Sun

PRICE RANGE: $$

NEIGHBORHOOD: Downtown

Popular steakhouse and oyster bar with a busy happy hour. Every time I visit this place I go back in time. Great selection of fresh oysters, beef dishes and signature desserts. Menu favorites include: Yellow fin tuna tartare and Filet Mignon. Nice menu of wine & beers.

CAFÉ BESALU
5909 24th Ave NW, Seattle, 206-789-1463
www.cafebesalu.com
CUISINE: Bakery, French
DRINKS: No Booze
SERVING: Breakfast, lunch, Wed - Sun
PRICE RANGE: $$
NEIGHBORHOOD: Central District
Be prepared for a line, as this place is busy. Owner James Miller (you'll se him working behind the counter) has earned a reputation for making the best croissant in Seattle, and to tell you the truth, his croissants are better than most of the ones you'll find in Paris. But it's not just the croissants—there's a wide variety of excellent pastries and great-smelling coffee.

CANLIS
2576 Aurora Ave N, Seattle, 206-283-3313
www.canlis.com
CUISINE: American; Pacific Northwest
DRINKS: Full Bar
SERVING: Dinner nightly except Sunday when it's closed
PRICE RANGE: $$$$
NEIGHBORHOOD: Westlake
Canlis offers a menu of contemporary Northwest cuisine for a fine dining experience in an elegant house from the mid-1950s (that makes you think Doris Day and Rock Hudson lived there while shooting a movie) overlooking the romantic lights running along Lake Union. Canlis features a variety of prix fixe menus (3 courses, 4 courses or a 7-course tasting menu with or without wine pairings) including a Vegetarian Tasting Menu. Menu favorites include: Canlis soufflé and King Salmon (the waiter might be able to tell you exactly where that salmon was caught). The sommelier can explain all the varieties of wines from Washington State—they have an excellent selection on the 100-page list. Bar offers an extensive selection of Scotches and bourbons. Reservations recommended.

THE CAPITAL GRILLE
THE COBB BUILDING
1301 Fourth Ave, Seattle, 206-382-0900
www.thecapitalgrille.com
CUISINE: Steakhouse, American
DRINKS: Full bar
SERVING: Mon – Fri lunch and dinner, Sat- Sun dinner only
PRICE RANGE: $$$
NEIGHBORHOOD: Downtown
Located in the historic Cobb Building, this classic steakhouse offers an impressive menu that also includes creative seafood dishes. Here you'll also find an award-winning wine list. Menu favorites include: Kona steak and Seared Sirloin and lobster tails. Free valet parking.

CASCINA SPINASSE
1531 14th Ave, Seattle, 206-251-7673
www.spinasse.com
CUISINE: Italian
DRINKS: Full bar
SERVING: Dinner daily
PRICE RANGE: $$$
NEIGHBORHOOD: Capitol Hill
This Italian eatery offers a menu of traditional cuisine from the Piedmont region of Northern Italy. Chef Jason Stratton features

a menu of simple, refined dishes, and delicious pastas. Extensive wine list. Menu favorites include: Ravioli di agnello (Lamb filled ravioli) and Pork ribs. Great place for a special occasion dinner.

CHANDLER'S CRABHOUSE
901 Fairview Ave, Seattle, 206-223-2722
www.schwartzbros.com/chandlers-crabhouse/
CUISINE: Seafood, Live/Raw Food
DRINKS: Full bar
SERVING: Mon- Fri lunch and dinner, Sat – Sun brunch and dinner
PRICE RANGE: $$$
NEIGHBORHOOD: South Lake Union
Located on historic South Lake Union, this iconic restaurant offers the ultimate Seattle crab experience with eight varieties of crab and 20 different crab dishes. Menu favorites include: Dungeness Crab (found locally) and Grilled Columbia River King Salmon. Desserts include: Chandler's Signature Key Lime Pie and Crème Brulee.

COPPERLEAF RESTAURANT
AT CEDARBROOK LODGE
18525 36th Ave, Seattle, 206-901-9268
www.cedarbrooklodge.com
CUISINE: American (New)
DRINKS: Full bar
SERVING: Lunch, and dinner
PRICE RANGE: $$$
NEIGHBORHOOD: Central District
Located in the lobby of the Cedarbrook Lodge 20 minutes outside town, this intimate restaurant offers a menu that features farm-to-table locally and regionally sourced foods. Menu favorites include: Anderson Ranch Spring Lamb and Sitka Bay King Salmon. The restaurant features a large wood-burning outdoor fireplace. Bar offers a nice selection of wines from local wineries.

DAHLIA LOUNGE
2001 4th Ave, Seattle, 206-682-4142
www.tomdouglas.com/index.php?page=dahlia-lounge
CUISINE: American, Seafood
DRINKS: Full bar
SERVING: Lunch, dinner, brunch
PRICE RANGE: $$$
NEIGHBORHOOD: Belltown

In this very dark hideaway with its intimate booths and lanterns hanging from the ceiling providing just about the only light, Chef Brock Johnson offers a creative "Asian infused" menu of Northwest cuisine. Menu favorites include: Neah Bay marble king salmon and Dungeness Crab cake. Delicious dessert selections like their famous Coconut Cream Pie. Oh, and don't forget the doughnuts that come to you fresh from the fryer and served with vanilla mascarpone and a seasonal jam.

DAMN THE WEATHER

116 1st Ave South, Seattle, 206-946-1283
www.damntheweather.com
CUISINE: American
DRINKS: Full Bar
SERVING: Dinner nightly
PRICE RANGE: $$
NEIGHBORHOOD: Pioneer Square
This upscale eatery offers a unique menu and serves excellent
craft cocktails made by experts of mixology. Menu favorites
include: Beef Heart tartare served with chicken-fat fries, and the
Pasta & Grains spaghetti. Nice assortment of sandwiches. Menu
changes frequently.

DANIEL'S BROILER

809 Fairview Place N, Seattle, 206-621-8262

www.schwartzbros.com/locations/daniels-broiler-lake-union/
CUISINE: Steakhouse
DRINKS: Full Bar
SERVING: Dinner nightly
PRICE RANGE: $$$$
NEIGHBORHOOD: Lake Union
This world-class steakhouse serves USDA Prime Steak exclusively. Other specials include North Pacific King Salmon and Lobster tails. Guests can enjoy waterfront dining with great views of Lake Union. Outdoor dining weather permitting. Live music.

DELANCEY
1415 NW 70th St, Seattle, 206-838-1960
www.delanceyseattle.com
CUISINE: Pizza
DRINKS: Full Bar
SERVING: Dinner
PRICE RANGE: $$
NEIGHBORHOOD: Phinney Ridge
This is Brandon Pettit and Molly Wizenberg's wood-fire pizza project. Delicious pizzas and a great selection of wines. If there's still room for dessert try the salted chocolate chip cookie served warm.

DICK'S DRIVE-IN
111 NE 45th St, Seattle, 206-323-1300
115 Broadway Ave E, Seattle, 206-323-1300
9208 Holman Rd NW, Seattle, 206-783-5233
12325 30th Ave NE, Seattle, 206-363-7777
500 Queen Anne Ave N, Seattle, 206-285-5155
www.ddir.com
CUISINE: Fast food, Burgers
DRINKS: Full bar
SERVING: Breakfast, lunch, dinner, late night
PRICE RANGE: $
NEIGHBORHOOD: Central District
This is a no-frills drive-in style eatery that features a typical menu of thin, griddled burgers, fries, shakes, and ice cream. If you don't like burgers you're out of luck.

DIN TAI FUNG
2621 NE 46th St, Seattle, 206-525-0958
www.dintaifungusa.com
CUISINE: Taiwanese, Shanghainese, Dim Sum
DRINKS: Full bar
SERVING: Lunch, and dinner
PRICE RANGE: $$
NEIGHBORHOOD: University District
The New York Times picked this place as one of the to ten
restaurants in the world. This restaurant specializes in dumplings.
Menu favorites include: Juicy Pork Dumplings and Soy Noodle
Salad. Vegetarian and Gluten-Free items available.

EL GAUCHO
2505 1st Ave, Seattle, 206-728-1337
www.elgaucho.com
CUISINE: Steaks/Seafood
DRINKS: Full Bar
SERVING: Lunch & Dinner
PRICE RANGE: $$
NEIGHBORHOOD: Belltown
Upscale steakhouse offers a romantic experience complete with
tuxedoed staff. A dimly lit eatery that takes its steak seriously
and sets a mood for fine dining including live jazz on the piano.

ELLIOTT'S OYSTER HOUSE

1201 Alaskan Way, Pier 56, Seattle, 206-623-4340
www.elliottsoysterhouse.com
CUISINE: Seafood, Live/Raw Food
DRINKS: Full bar
SERVING: Lunch and dinner daily
PRICE RANGE: $$$
NEIGHBORHOOD: Waterfront
This seafood eatery is known for their seafood specialties like
the Dungeness crab and Alaskan halibut. Menu favorites include:
Grilled Scampi Prawn Risotto and Dungeness Crab Cakes.
Located on Pier 56 since 1975, this vibrant waterfront eatery is
popular for lunch, dinner, and happy hour. Oysters are $1 each
from 3-4 p.m.

FRANK'S OYSTER HOUSE & CHAMPAGNE PARLOR

2616 NE 55th St (bet. N 26th Ave & N 27th Ave), Seattle, 206-
525-0220
www.franksoysterhouse.com
CUISINE: American, Seafood
DRINKS: Full bar
SERVING: Lunch, and dinner
PRICE RANGE: $$$
NEIGHBORHOOD: Ravenna
Grab a seat in one of the Spartan wood booths lining one wall.
Or take a tufted white barstool in this combination restaurant

and lounge, both rooms are elegant if you like the lumberjack look. The Champagnes will go well with the oysters harvested by Taylor Shellfish Farms. Menu favorites include: Maine lobster rolls, cornmeal fried oysters, baked oysters, Dungeness crab lettuce cups, potato cheddar gratin and Roasted Red Beet fettuccini. Great happy hour and Sunday brunch.

FLYING FISH
300 West Lake Ave, Seattle, 206-728-8595
www.flyingfishseattle.com
CUISINE: Seafood
DRINKS: Full bar
SERVING: Lunch, and dinner
PRICE RANGE: $$$
NEIGHBORHOOD: South Lake Union
This is a local favorite for seafood with a creative menu and a bar that offers a nice selection of Pacific Northwest wines and beers. They have an Oyster Frenzy Happy Hour where you can get oysters really cheap (in oyster season only). They also do an all-you-can-eat Oyster Frenzy every year in the Fall. Menu favorites include: Crispy Catfish, salt & pepper Alaskan king crab, wild Columbia River steelhead and Jerk Butter Soft Shell Crab.

HOMEGROWN

1531 Melrose Ave, Seattle, 206-682-0935
3416 Fremont Ave N, Seattle, 206-453-5232 (pickup only)
2201 Queen Anne Ave, Seattle, 206-217-4745
2nd Ave & Marion St, Seattle, 206-624-1329
208 Westlake Ave N, Seattle, 206-467-5391
www.eathomegrown.com
CUISINE: Sandwiches, Salads
DRINKS: Full bar
SERVING: Daily breakfast, lunch, and dinner
PRICE RANGE: $$
NEIGHBORHOODS: Capitol Hill, Fremont, Queen Anne,
Downtown, South Lake Union
This friendly eatery serves primarily salads and sandwiches.
They are quick to boast that they serve "sustainable sandwiches,"
using locally sourced and seasonal ingredients. Lots of Google
employee eat here. Favorites include: Peanut Butter & Jelly;
BBQ Pork with ancho chile BBQ sauce & creamy bok choy
slaw); Cream Cheese & Veggie; roast pork with coffe e rub &
cayenne.

IL CORVO

217 James St (bet. 2nd & 3rd Aves), Seattle, 206-538-0999
www.ilcorvopasta.com
CUISINE: Italian
DRINKS: Beer & Wine
SERVING: Lunch only Monday-Friday; closed weekends
PRICE RANGE: $
NEIGHBORHOOD: Pioneer Square
This very popular eatery serves great pasta. Menu favorites
include: Wild boar tagliatelle, rigatoni alla Bolognese,
homemade Coppa (the long version is "Capocollo," a cooked
salami made from a cut from behind the pig's head that is cured
in brine, rolled in pepper, chili and fennel seed, usually sliced
and put into a pasta dish). Their chalkboard menu lists only 3
items daily, though they do have a few antipasti selections like
house made focaccia, prosciutto, salami plate, spicy chickpea
salad. Note: this is a narrow little spot that serves lunch only, but
well worth your time if you can squeeze it into your schedule. If
you don't want to wait, show up for a late lunch at 1:30.

IL FORNAIO CUCINA ITALIANA
600 Pine St, Seattle, 206-264-0994
www.ilfornaio.com
CUISINE: Italian, Deli
DRINKS: Full bar
SERVING: Lunch and dinner daily
PRICE RANGE: $$$
NEIGHBORHOOD: Downtown
This authentic Italian deli is like taking a journey through Italy.
Great menu of Italian fare complemented by a great selection of
regional wines. Menu favorites include: Scaloppine ai Carciofi
e Limone (veal sautéed with sliced artichokes) and Grigliata di
Pesce Misto (Mixed grill of salmon, calamari, scallops, whitefish
and prawns). Gluten-Free menu available upon request.

IL TERRAZZO CARMINE

411 First Ave. S., Seattle, 206-467-7797

www.ilterrazzocarmine.com

CUISINE: Italian

DRINKS: Full bar

SERVING: Lunch/Dinner Mon – Fri; Dinner only on Sat; closed Sun

PRICE RANGE: $$$

NEIGHBORHOOD: Pioneer Square

When you've had your fill of the excellent seafood specialties available in Seattle (if that's possible), get your butt over to this popular eatery that has attracted crowds since 1984, where you'll find classic Italian fare in a welcoming atmosphere. Menu picks include: Rigatoni Bolognese and Spaghetti alla vongole.

IVAR'S SALMON HOUSE

401 NE Northlake Way, Seattle, 206-632-0767

www.ivars.com/

CUISINE: Seafood

DRINKS: Full Bar

SERVING: Lunch & Dinner

PRICE RANGE: $$

NEIGHBORHOOD: Wellingford

A local seafood chain offering counter service with a reputation for fresh fried fish and chowders. Favorites include the fish and chips and the chowders are a must.

JACK'S FISH SPOT

1514 Pike Pl, Seattle, 206-467-0514

www.jacksfishspot.com

CUISINE: Seafood Market/Seafood

DRINKS: No Booze

SERVING: Lunch (11a.m. – 5 p.m.)

PRICE RANGE: $

NEIGHBORHOOD: Downtown

Great Seattle institution known for fresh seafood, live crab and shellfish tanks. Locals flock to the stand-up seafood bar in the back, and I suggest you do as well. Just go back there and eat standing up. Try the clam chowder – it's the best. Great selections like Fish tacos with garlic fries. Remember, you're here for the food, not the ambiance.

JOHN HOWIE STEAK
11111 NE Eighth St, Seattle, 425-440-0880
www.johnhowiesteak.com
CUISINE: Steakhouse, American
DRINKS: Full bar
SERVING: Lunch, and dinner
PRICE RANGE: $$$$
NEIGHBORHOOD: Bellevue
Double wooden doors open into the dark-wooded interior of
this steakhouse that offers an upscale dining experience and a
selection of some of the world's best steaks. The elegant dining
room has an interesting textured wall treatment and slender
slender light fixtures dangling from the ceiling, the light partially
diffused by parchment paper. The bar has a blue and white light
emanating from beneath, which lightens things up a bit. Menu
favorites include: Spicy Habanero Butter and Australian Lobster
Tails. Delicious steaks served tableside (as are the Bananas
Foster). Vegetarian selections available. Impressive wine list.
Reservations recommended.

JOULE
3506 Stone Way North, Seattle, 206-632-5685
www.joulerestaurant.com
CUISINE: Asian Fusion/Korean
DRINKS: Full bar

SERVING: Dinner Nightly; Lunch on Sat & Sun
PRICE RANGE: $$
NEIGHBORHOOD: Wallingford
From celebrated husband and wife cooking team Rachel Yang and Seif Chirchi, this popular eatery with the outdoor fire pit has not only gained a local following but has received national media attention. Enjoy a showcase of unconventional cuts of beef treated with things like anchovy miso or a sumac rub. Totally unconventional and totally delicious. You must try the rice cakes with chorizo. The tasting menu offers a nice assortment.

KEDAI MAKAN
1802 Bellevue Ave, Seattle, 206-556-2560
www.kedaimakansea.com
CUISINE: Malaysian food stand
DRINKS: No
SERVING: Daily dinner from 4 p.m. to 2 a.m.
PRICE RANGE: $
NEIGHBORHOOD: Capitol Hill
This Malaysian take-out joint has a few seats by the window for those who care to dine in. A favorite of the late-night crowd, here you'll find a new menu daily that usually features eight dishes with a noodle and fried rice dish. Menu favorites include: Char Siu (Roast pork) and Pork Belly in herbal broth. On the late-

night menu you can get the Malaysian Burger, topped with an egg and a cabbage-chili mix giving it a sweet & savory taste.

KINGS HARDWARE
5225 Ballard Ave NW, Seattle, 206-782-0027
www.kingsballard.com
CUISINE: American
DRINKS: Full bar
SERVING: Daily breakfast, lunch, and dinner
PRICE RANGE: $$
NEIGHBORHOOD: Ballard
Located in historic Ballard, this pub offers a menu of standard bar cuisine. Creative burger selections like the After School Special, a burger topped with peanut butter and bacon. Patio dining available when weather permits.

LOCAL 360
2234 1st Ave, Seattle, 206-441-9360
www.local360.org/
CUISINE: Modern American
DRINKS: Full bar
SERVING: Lunch & Dinner; breakfast on weekends
PRICE RANGE: $$
NEIGHBORHOOD: Belltown
Located in the heart of downtown, this sustainable café focuses on local sourcing, to the extreme point that they pride themselves n serving items found within 360 miles of Seattle, whether it's booze or pig ears. Great spot for weekend brunch. Menu favorites include: Fried Chicken & Waffles with Maple Pepper Jelly and for dessert the molten peanut butter bon bons. (Peanut butter balls are inserted into a brioche crumb roll and then fried before being put on top of a dollop of blackberry preserves. They serve it with a shot glass of raw milk. Yum! This'll take you back to the farm. Nice happy hour.

LITTLE UNCLE
1523 East Madison, Seattle, 206-549-6507
www.littleuncleseattle.com
CUISINE: Thai
DRINKS: No
SERVING: Mon - Fri lunch

PRICE RANGE: $
NEIGHBORHOOD: Capitol Hill
This Thai take-out joint was founded by chefs PK and Wiley
Frank and inspired by the family restaurants of Thailand. Here
you'll find dishes like steamed pork cheek buns, khao soi, and
phad thai. Order online before dropping by for faster service.

THE LONDON PLANE
300 Occidental Ave S, Seattle, 206-624-1374
www.thelondonplaneseattle.com
CUISINE: Café / Breakfast
DRINKS: Beer & Wine Only
SERVING: Breakfast, Lunch & Dinner
PRICE RANGE: $$
NEIGHBORHOOD: Pioneer Square
A friendly local hangout in the heart of Pioneer Square that's a
combination wine bar and store (fresh flowers, anyone?) with a
menu of small plates sets in a building going back over a century.
Get beautifully packaged soaps, spices sold by the pound, Libeco
tea towels from Belgium. Great place for brunch (poached eggs
on homemade sourdough bread, seasonal salads) and vegetarian
fare. From your vantage point here you overlook Occidental
Park. Traffic is barred from this section, so it's quite a gorgeous
view. Flower-arranging classes and cooking classes as well.

LUC
2800 E Madison St, Seattle, 206-328-6645
www.thechefinthehat.com/luc-restaurant-seattle/
CUISINE: American (New) / French
DRINKS: Full Bar
SERVING: Dinner nightly, Lunch weekends
PRICE RANGE: $$
NEIGHBORHOOD: Capitol Hill
Chef Thierry Rautureau offers a creative menu of French-
American fare. Great corner café that attracts a lively happy hour
crowd. Great stop for weekend brunch.

MAMNOON
1508 Melrose Ave, Seattle, 206-906-9606
www.mamnoonrestaurant.com
CUISINE: Lebanese, Persian and Iranian

DRINKS: Full bar
SERVING: Tues – Sun lunch and dinner, Mon closed
PRICE RANGE: $$$
NEIGHBORHOOD: Capitol Hill
This modern style restaurant offers a variety of Middle Eastern cuisines. Menu favorites include: Baghali Polow (Braised lamb shank) and Shish Taouk (Chicken). Order at the sidewalk counter or dine inside.

MANOLIN
3621 Stone Way N, Seattle, 206-294-3331
www.manolinseattle.com
CUISINE: Seafood
DRINKS: Full Bar
SERVING: Dinner; closed Mondays
PRICE RANGE: $$
Relaxed eatery with a nice menu of New American cuisine and delicious seafood in what is surely one of the top spots in all of Seattle. The nautical motif is predominant, and everything is focused around the U-shaped bar where top cocktail craftsmen shake their drinks while cooks man the wood-burning grills behind them. Menu favorites include Smoked Arctic char served on top of their homemade sour cream, rockfish ceviche, grilled halibut and Tea Poached Squid. Courtyard & patio. No reservations.

MARINATION MA KAI
1660 Harbor Ave SW, Seattle, 206-328-8226
www.marinationmobile.com
CUISINE: Korean, Hawaiian, Asian Fusion
DRINKS: Full bar
SERVING: Lunch, Dinner, Closed Sun
PRICE RANGE: $
NEIGHBORHOOD: Harbor
This casual dining establishment, situated right on the dock where the water taxi is located, serves up Hawaiian-Korean cuisine that features their famous tacos that come in four flavors: spicy pork, kalbi beef, ginger miso chicken, and sexy tofu. Cool off with their famous Hawaiian Shaved Ice. Beachside location with indoor and patio dining.

MASHIKO

4725 California Ave SW, Seattle, 206-935-4339
www.mashikorestaurant.com
CUISINE: Japanese, Sushi Bars
DRINKS: Beer & Wine
SERVING: Dinner nightly
PRICE RANGE: $$$
NEIGHBORHOOD: Fairmount Park; West Seattle
Open since 2009, this is Seattle's first sustainable sushi bar. Here you'll find a great menu of fresh items like raw oyster, ahi poke, scallop nigiri with lemon and tobiko. Menu includes several Omakase Course Meals – Chef's Choices. Get the hard-to-find "geoduck" (a huge clam shaped like a club foot) if it's in season. Nice selection of sakes and wines.

MATADOR

2221 NW Market St, Seattle, 206-297-2855
www.matadorseattle.com
CUISINE: Tex-Mex
DRINKS: Full bar
SERVING: Lunch, and dinner
PRICE RANGE: $$
NEIGHBORHOOD: Ballard
Here you'll find a menu featuring fresh, gourmet Tex-Mex cuisine. Menu favorites include: Shredded Chicken Taco plate and Grilled Stuffed Jalapenos. The bar offers creative cocktails and a selection of over 100 varieties of tequila.

MATT'S IN THE MARKET
94 Pike St #32, Seattle, 206-467-7909
www.mattsinthemarket.com
CUISINE: American
DRINKS: Full bar
SERVING: Lunch and dinner
PRICE RANGE: $$$
NEIGHBORHOOD: Downtown
If you're tired of watching the street artists perform outside the original Starbucks, cross the street and relax here. Located on the third floor of the Corner Market Building, this eatery offers great views of Elliot Bay. Chef Shane Ryan's seasonal menu features Pacific NW cuisine with seafood being a specialty. Menu favorites include: Halibut in Pesto sauce, cornmeal-crusted catfish sandwich and Wild Boar Chop. Happy Hour specials.

MAXIMILIEN
81 Pike St, Seattle, 206-682-7270
www.maximilienrestaurant.com
CUISINE: French
DRINKS: Full bar
SERVING: Lunch, dinner
PRICE RANGE: $$
NEIGHBORHOOD: Downtown
Located in the heart of historic Pike Place Market, this romantic French restaurant offers a creative, seasonal menu. At happy

hour you can get a big bowl of mussels steamed in wine for just a few dollars. Menu favorites include: Duck Confit and Morue Charbonnière â l'Estragon - a pan seared sablefish. For dessert choose the sampler which allows you to taste four of their most popular desserts.

METROPOLITAN GRILL
820 Second Ave, Seattle, 206-624-3287
www.themetropolitangrill.com
CUISINE: American, Steakhouse
DRINKS: Full bar
SERVING: Mon – Fri lunch and dinner, Sat –Sun dinner only
PRICE RANGE: $$$$
NEIGHBORHOOD: Downtown
Located in the historic Marion Building, this classic steakhouse offers an upscale dining experience from the moment you're greeted by the tuxedo-clad maître d'. The menu features classics like: filet mignon, New York peppercorn steak, porterhouse and Chateaubriand carved at your table. The 60-foot black marble bar is a popular meeting spot and the martini is the house specialty. The bar also features an impressive wine list.

MILLER'S GUILD
HOTEL MAX

612 Stewart St (b/t 7th Ave & 6th Ave), Seattle, 206-443-3663
www.millersguild.com
www.hotelmaxseattle.com
CUISINE: American, Steakhouse
DRINKS: Full bar
SERVING: Daily breakfast, lunch, and dinner
PRICE RANGE: $$$
NEIGHBORHOOD: Denny Triangle

Located in the Hotel Max, Miller's Guild is built around a 9-foot custom wood-fired grill that grills not only the superior bone-in cuts of beef but the veggies as well. For a steak place, I can suggest you do yourself a favor and get aside of grilled veggies. You'll like the ruggedly handsome design that reveals the history of the 1926 building as well as custom furnishings created by Seattle carpenters, metalworkers and masons. Chef Jason Wilson offers an impressive menu that includes 75-day dry aged beef. The bar serves inventive craft cocktails and features a wine list of crafted wines from the Pacific Northwest. Menu favorites include: Hearth Roasted Scallops, Bavette steak & eggs, braised octopus and smoked bone marrow and Wild King Salmon. The pastries here are superb like the cookie-dough cheesecake. Popular for Sunday brunch.

MILSTEAD & CO
900 N 34th St, Seattle, 206-659-4814
www.milsteadandco.com
CUISINE: Coffee
DRINKS: No Booze
SERVING: Open daily until 6 p.m.
PRICE RANGE: $
Specialty coffeehouse offering a variety of coffees including: Heart, Kuma, Bows & Arrows, and Wrecking Ball. This is a favorite of the true coffee connoisseur.

MONSOON RESTAURANT
615 19th Ave, Seattle, 206-325-2111
www.monsoonrestaurants.com
CUISINE: Vietnamese, Asian Fusion, Dim Sum
DRINKS: Beer and Wine only
SERVING: Mon – Fri lunch and dinner, Sun and Sat Dim Sum brunch and dinner
PRICE RANGE: $$$
NEIGHBORHOOD: Capitol Hill
This unique eatery offers a menu of Vietnamese cuisine with a Northwest twist. Great wine selection. Menu favorites include: Drunken Chicken and Prawns & Yellow Curry. Good happy hour with drink specials.

NISHINO
3130 E Madison St, Seattle, 206-322-5800
www.nishinorestaurant.com
CUISINE: Sushi / Japanese
DRINKS: Full Bar
SERVING: Dinner
PRICE RANGE: $$
NEIGHBORHOOD: Washington Park
An upscale Japanese eatery known for its omakase menu and inventive sushi. Great place for dinner with friends.

ODDFELLOWS
1525 10th Ave, Seattle, 206-325-0807
www.oddfellowscafe.com/
CUISINE: American
DRINKS: Full Bar

SERVING: Breakfast, Lunch & Dinner
PRICE RANGE: $$
NEIGHBORHOOD: Capitol Hill
A locals' favorite for lunch or brunch, this stylish eatery located next to the Elliott Bay Book Co. offers a creative menu of seasonal American fare like deviled eggs, mac n cheese and a cherry bread pudding that's wonderful. Great craft cocktails.

OSTERIA LA SPIGA
1429 12th Ave, Seattle, 206-323-8881
www.laspiga.com
CUISINE: Italian
DRINKS: Full bar
SERVING: Mon – Fri lunch and dinner, Sat – Sun dinner only
PRICE RANGE: $$
NEIGHBORHOOD: Capitol Hill
This comfortable neighborhood spot is a favorite of locals and tourists. Known for its authentic, northern Italian cuisine. Menu favorites include: Ortelli agli Asparagi (Asparagus filled tortelli) and Lasagne di Melanzane. Gigantic wine list.

PORCHLIGHT COFFEE & RECORDS
1517 14th Ave, Seattle, 206-329-5461
www.porchlightcoffee.com/
CUISINE: Coffee
DRINKS: No Booze
SERVING: Open daily until 6 p.m. – weekends – 5 p.m.
PRICE RANGE: $

This unique coffeehouse/record shop combo attracts locals and hipsters. The coffeehouse offers coffees, beer, sandwiches, bagels and pastries. (The do-nuts are from Mighty-O.)The record shop sells new and used vinyl.

PURPLE CAFÉ AND WINE BAR
1225 Fourth Ave, Seattle, 206-829-2280
www.purplecafe.com
CUISINE: American
DRINKS: Full bar
SERVING: Lunch and dinner daily
PRICE RANGE: $$$
NEIGHBORHOOD: Downtown
The Purple Café and Wine Bar is a great lunch destination. Wine list featuring global wines, 80 by the glass and 600 varieties of bottles. Menu favorites include: Spiced Rub lamb chops and Pork Porterhouse with lobster mac & cheese. Nice dessert selection.

RAIN SHADOW MEATS
1531 Melrose Ave, Ste C, Seattle, 206-467-6328
www.rainshadowmeats.com
CUISINE: Meat Market, Sandwich
DRINKS: Wine and beer only
SERVING: Daily 10 am – 7pm
PRICE RANGE: $$
NEIGHBORHOOD: Capitol Hill

Here you'll find the best well sourced meat in the city and house made Charcuteiere. Very much like an old school butcher shop. Menu favorites include: Corned Beef Hash and Romesco Beef Sandwich. Dining is communal and it's always busy so expect a wait at lunch.

RAY'S BOATHOUSE
6049 Seaview Ave, Seattle, 206-789-3770
www.rays.com/boathouse
CUISINE: American, Seafood
DRINKS: Full bar
SERVING: Dinner daily
PRICE RANGE: $$$
NEIGHBORHOOD: Sunset Hill
This café is a popular spot for locals and tourists with plenty of outdoor seating in the summer. The menu features American classics like burgers, chicken, seafood, and vegetarian choices. Menu favorites include: Snow Crab and Salmon Salad.

RED MILL BURGERS
312 N 67th St, Seattle, 206-783-6362
www.redmillburgers.com
CUISINE: Burgers
DRINKS: No Booze
SERVING: Lunch, dinner

PRICE RANGE: $ / **CASH ONLY**
NEIGHBORHOOD: Phinney Ridge
While the burgers at **Dick's Drive-In** are thin like fast food burgers, here they are thick and juicy quarter-pounders with a smoky flavor from the mayo-based Mill sauce they use. This is definitely a place for burger lovers with choices like the Bleu Cheese n' Bacon Burger. For a perfect combo order a burger with fries and one of their delicious chocolate malts. Cash only.

REVEL
403 N 36th St (bet. N Francis Ave & Phinney Ave), Seattle, 206-547-2040
www.revelseattle.com
CUISINE: Asian Fusion
DRINKS: Full Bar
SERVING: Lunch, Dinner, & Brunch
PRICE RANGE: $$
NEIGHBORHOOD: Fremont
Not your typical Korean BBQ joint, this eatery offers a creative Asian Fusion menu in a comfortable atmosphere featuring an open kitchen and long communal tables where you can watch them work. Menu favorites include: Pork Belly Pancake and Short Rib Dumplings (any dish featuring their short ribs is beyond excellent). Vegetarian options available.

RN74 SEATTLE
1433 Fourth Ave, Seattle, 206-456-7474
www.michaelmina.net/restaurants/locations/rnwa.php
CUISINE: American, French
DRINKS: Full bar
SERVING: Mon- Fri lunch and dinner, Sat dinner only, Sun closed
PRICE RANGE: $$$
NEIGHBORHOOD: Downtown
Designed to give customers the feel of a vintage train station, Chef Michael Mina's entry into the Seattle dining scene was named after Route National 74. A divider is made up of railroad lanterns. The wine bar is right in the middle of things, its walls covered with the name of 100 wines offered on the market list. A railroad station sign flips occasionally to highlight last bottles offered. This urban wine bar and restaurant offers a menu

featuring American and regional French cuisine. They also offer an extensive wine list with French wines as well as wines from local wineries in Washington and Oregon with a selection of over 40 wines by the glass. Menu favorites include: Ahi Tuna Tartare, Painted Hills beef, a 35-day aged New York Oscar and Rn74 Beef Bourguignon.

ROCKCREEK SEAFOOD & SPIRITS
4300 Fremont Ave N (bet. 44th St & 43rd St), Seattle, 206-557-7532
www.rockcreekseattle.com
CUISINE: Seafood
DRINKS: Full Bar
SERVING: Dinner from 4 daily; Brunch on weekends from 9 a.m.
PRICE RANGE: $$$
NEIGHBORHOOD: Fremont
This casual seafood eatery offers a variety of plate sizes to fit any budget. The high-ceilinged loft-like atmosphere is crowd friendly. The bar stools (no backs) are made of hard wood, as are the tables. No real decoration of any kind. It's all about the food. Seasonal menu. Menu favorites include: Chili braised and grilled octopus; several kinds of oysters (both raw and cooked several ways—my favorite is the Brock-a-Fella, with bacon, shallots, thyme and tamarind butter); oil-poached local albacore; Grilled Hawaiian ono with Marconi Almonds.

SALTY'S ON ALKI BEACH

1936 Harbor Ave, Seattle, 206-937-1600
www.saltys.com/seattle/
CUISINE: Seafood, Steakhouse
DRINKS: Full bar
SERVING: Mon – Fri lunch and dinner, Sat – Sun brunch and
dinner
PRICE RANGE: $$$
NEIGHBORHOOD: West Seattle
With great views of Elliott Bay and Seattle's skyline, this favorite
seafood eatery features an award-winning menu. Menu favorites
include: Yellowfish Tuna and Angus Beef Natural Steak. Great
choice for weekend brunch. Happy Hour menu is a locals'
favorite. Free limo service from most downtown hotels.

SALUMI

309 3rd Ave S, Seattle, (b/t S 2nd Ave Extended & Main St),
206-621-8772
www.salumicuredmeats.com
CUISINE: Sandwiches/Meat Shop
DRINKS: Beer & Wine Only
SERVING: Lunch
PRICE RANGE: $$
NEIGHBORHOOD: Pioneer Square
Small eatery and meat shop offering limited seating. This is for
fans of salami and other artisanal Italian cured meats. Only the
finest served here. You won't forget it. Great sandwiches.

SEATTLE CULINARY ACADEMY

1701 Broadway BE2120, Seattle, 206-934-5424

www.seattlecentral.edu

CUISINE: American (New)

DRINKS: No Booze

SERVING: Lunch; closed Mon & Fri; classes start in September, with lunch service beginning early October.

PRICE RANGE: $

NEIGHBORHOOD: Capitol Hill

A very cheap lunch-only eatery run by students of the Academy offers a creative menu of small plates (lemon thyme panna cotta with Dungeness crab, buttermilk soup with pickled cherries), sandwiches, salads, canapés, patés, and melt-in-your-mouth desserts. This is the oldest culinary school west of the Mississippi. They teach their students about sustainability and even send them to work on Skagit Valley Farms for hands-on experience. These kids go on to work for some of the best chefs in the country.

SERIOUS PIE

316 Virginia St, Seattle, 206-838-7388

www.seriouspieseattle.com

CUISINE: Pizza

DRINKS: Beer & Wine

SERVING: Lunch, dinner

PRICE RANGE: $$

NEIGHBORHOOD: Belltown

As the name implies, this is a place for serious pizza lovers. Here you'll find wood-fired thin-crust and slightly charred gourmet pizzas served at communal tables. (I like the sweet fennel and sausage pie.) Bar offers wine & beer and great happy hour from 3 to 5 p.m. weekdays.

SITKA & SPRUCE

1531 Melrose Ave, Seattle, 206-324-0662

www.sitkaandspruce.com

CUISINE: American

DRINKS: Beer & Wine

SERVING: Lunch, and dinner

PRICE RANGE: $$$

NEIGHBORHOOD: Capitol Hill

Located in the back of the **Melrose Market**, in a building that once housed an auto shop. This place looks like the kitchen of a country house. But it's one of the hottest restaurants in town. The restaurant features a brick wood-burning oven showcased in the open kitchen with a Northwest-ingredient-driven seasonal menu. Menu favorites include: Fireplace Roasted Quail and Pacific Halibut. Great choice for Sunday Brunch.

SKILLET DINER
1400 E Union St, Seattle, 206-512-2001
www.skilletstreetfood.com
CUISINE: American, Diner
DRINKS: Full bar
SERVING: Daily breakfast, lunch, and dinner
PRICE RANGE: $$
NEIGHBORHOOD: Central District; Capitol Hill
This favorite neighborhood diner offers a creative menu featuring locally sourced ingredients. Like most diners, this place offers a great breakfast menu and menu favorites include Chicken Fried Steak, grilled peanut butter & jelly sandwiches and Chicken and Waffles.

SKYCITY AT THE NEEDLE
400 Broad St, Seattle, 206-905-2100
www.spaceneedle.com
CUISINE: American
DRINKS: Full bar
SERVING: Mon – Fri lunch and dinner, Sat- Sun brunch and dinner

PRICE RANGE: $$$
NEIGHBORHOOD: Lower Queen Anne
Located 500 feet about the ground, this restaurant is popular
among the tourists for the rotating view of downtown Seattle.
Chef Jeff Maxfield offers a varied menu featuring locally sourced
ingredients. Menu favorites include: Tai Snapper and Chatham
Strait Black Cod.

SPINASSE
1531 14th Ave, Seattle, 206-251-7673
www.spinasse.com
CUISINE: Italian
DRINKS: Full Bar
SERVING: Dinner
PRICE RANGE: $$$
NEIGHBORHOOD: Capitol Hill
Northern Italian fare is the specialty in this friendly place that
emphasizes local ingredients. The open kitchen adds character
to this charming spot. Menu favorites include: Lemon crispy
chicken and Hair thin spaghetti served half with butter and
cheese and the other half with ragu. There's also the hand-cut
egg pasta with fried sage and butter. Anti-carb? Get the salmon
wrapped in chard.

STAPLE & FANCY MERCANTILE

4739 Ballard Ave, Seattle, 206-789-1200
www.ethanstowellrestaurants.com/stapleandfancy
CUISINE: Seafood, Italian
DRINKS: Full bar
SERVING: Dinner
PRICE RANGE: $$$
NEIGHBORHOOD: Ballard

This is the newest creation of celebrated Chef Ethan Stowell. Located in a renovated early 1900s building, this intimate restaurant offers a menu showcasing Ethan's Italian inspired cooking style. You can choose where you want to order from the "staple" menu or the "fancy" menu, which means the chef's choice prix fixe menu. Lots of the dishes are evocative of the sea, and I love that salty hint you find in so many of the dishes here. Menu favorites include: Striped Bass or Grilled Rabbit Leg. There's also the option of letting the waiter order for you (at a prix fixe). Wine list features Northwest labels.

STATESIDE

300 E Pike St, Seattle, 206-557-7273
www.statesideseattle.com
CUISINE: Vietnamese/French
DRINKS: Full Bar
SERVING: Dinner nightly, lunch weekdays
PRICE RANGE: $$

Modern eatery (located in what used to be an old parking garage—that concrete floor you're walking on dates back to 1910) offering a unique combination of French & Vietnamese fusion fare. Menu favorites include: Crispy Duck Fresh Rolls and Chili Cumin Pork Ribs. They have several unusual tropical style cocktails from the bar you might want to try.

STEELHEAD DINER
95 Pine St, Suite 17, Seattle, 206-625-0129
www.steelheaddiner.com
CUISINE: Seafood
DRINKS: Full bar
SERVING: Lunch and dinner daily
PRICE RANGE: $$
NEIGHBORHOOD: Downtown
This casual eatery offers a great menu from Chef Kevin Davis.
Menu favorites include: Grilled Alaskan Troll King Salmon and
Grilled Alaskan Halibut. The outdoor patio overlooks Post Alley,
the bustling city market. Creative dessert selections like the
Tiramisu Cheesecake.

TAYLOR SHELLFISH FARMS
1521 Melrose Ave, Seattle, 206-501-4321
www.taylorshellfishfarms.com/
CUISINE: Seafood Market, Raw Food
DRINKS: Beer & Wine
SERVING: Lunch, dinner
PRICE RANGE: $$
NEIGHBORHOOD: Capitol Hill
This is the original location that features a retail store. Great
menu of fresh oysters, local wines, beers and cider. Menu
favorites include: Smoked Salmon Plate, geoduck clams in
season, housemade chowders and Dungeness Crab Cooked,
Chilled, and Cracked. Closed Mondays.

TEN MERCER
10 Mercer St, Seattle, 206-691-3723
www.tenmercer.com
CUISINE: American
DRINKS: Full bar
SERVING: Dinner daily
PRICE RANGE: $$
NEIGHBORHOOD: Lower Queen Anne
This neighborhood restaurant offers a menu of world-class
cuisine. Menu favorites include: Pan Fried Trout and Seared
Petite Tenderloin Medallion. Here you can also enjoy creative
cocktails and select from an award winning wine list. Regular &
gluten-free menus. Located near regional theaters.

TOSHI'S TERIYAKI GRILL

16212 Bothell Everett Hwy, Mill Creek, 425-225-6420
www.toshisgrill.com
CUISINE: Japanese
DRINKS: No Booze
SERVING: Lunch, and dinner
PRICE RANGE: $
NEIGHBORHOOD: Capitol Hill
Open since 1979, this was the first teriyaki joint to open in the
Seattle area and this is the only location currently run by original
founder Toshi Kasahara. The simple menu offers a variety of
teriyaki including several chef's favorites. Menu favorites include
Chicken Katsu and Eggroll-Gyoza Combo.

TOULOUSE PETIT

601 Queen Anne Ave, Seattle, 206-432-9069
www.toulousepetit.com
CUISINE: Cajun/Creole
DRINKS: Full bar
SERVING: Daily breakfast, lunch, and dinner
PRICE RANGE: $$
NEIGHBORHOOD: Lower Queen Anne
This Seattle favorite offers an expansive menu with a variety of
menu choices including traditional Creole and French Quarter
items to traditional French dishes. The bar serves great cocktails
and offers a wine list focusing on Northwest and French labels.

TRACE

1112 Fourth Ave, Seattle, 206-264-6060
www.traceseattle.com
CUISINE: American, Sushi
DRINKS: Full bar
SERVING: Mon – Fri breakfast, lunch, and dinner, Sat – Sun brunch and dinner
PRICE RANGE: $$$
NEIGHBORHOOD: Downtown
Chef Steven Ariel offers diners a contemporary urban dining experience with a creative menu featuring regional specialties and adding an Asian touch. Menu favorites include: Sashimi Salad and Hanger steak. Creative desserts like Richter's Rhubarb Strawberry White Chocolate Trifle. The restaurant's bar serves handcrafted cocktails and wine from choice Washington State wineries. Sushi bar.

TRAVELERS THALI HOUSE

2524 Beacon Ave S (bet. Bayview St & Lander St), Seattle, (206) 329-6260
www.travelersthalihouse.com
CUISINE: Indian, Vegetarian
DRINKS: Beer & Wine
SERVING: Lunch, dinner, closed Mon & Tues
PRICE RANGE: $$

NEIGHBORHOOD: Beacon Hill

When you walk up the 6 steps to this little spot, you'll see each step has a single word written on it—all together they read, COOK WITH LOVE EAT WITH PASSION. Thali House is named after the word that refers to the platter that holds a variety of individual dishes combined to create a complete Indian meal. So here guests can order a variety of authentic Indian dishes including vegetarian choices. Here you can also find culinary herbs and spices, tea, sweets, and Indian groceries in their little market.

THE TRIPLE DOOR

216 Union St, Seattle, 206-838-4333

www.thetripledoor.net

CUISINE: Asian Fusion, Music venue

DRINKS: Full bar

SERVING: Dinner daily

PRICE RANGE: $$$

NEIGHBORHOOD: Downtown

This is a great restaurant and music venue that offers world-class entertainment and award-winning cuisine. Menu favorites include: Panang Beef Curry and Wild Ginger Fragrant Duck. In the mainstage theatre you'll find national and international touring acts while the lounge features an eclectic variety of live music. No cover.

TULIO RESTAURANT
Hotel Vintage Park

1100 Fifth Ave, Seattle, 206-624-5500

www.tulio.com

CUISINE: Italian

DRINKS: Full bar

SERVING: Mon – Fri breakfast, lunch, and dinner, Sat – Sun brunch and dinner

PRICE RANGE: $$$

NEIGHBORHOOD: Downtown

This popular Italian trattoria offers an impressive menu from Chef Walter Pisano. Menu favorites include: Kurobuta Pork Shank and Washington Lamb Sirloin. Great place for a power lunch or a pre-theater dinner. Gluten-free, vegetarian and vegan menus available. Great desserts like the warm chocolate pudding cake served with toasted meringue and raspberry caramel sauce.

VICTROLA COFFEE ROASTERS

310 E Pike St, Seattle, 206-325-6080
www.victrolacoffee.com
CUISINE: Coffee
DRINKS: No Booze
SERVING: Open daily until 8 p.m.
PRICE RANGE: $
Vintage-themed coffeehouse with a nice menu of global coffees, snacks and pastries. Dog friendly. Free Wi-Fi.

VIF WINE/COFFEE

4401 Fremont Ave N, Seattle, 206-557-7357
www.vifseattle.com
CUISINE: Cafe
DRINKS: Beer & Wine Only
SERVING: Open daily until 7 p.m.; closed Mondays
PRICE RANGE: $$
Café with a menu of New American bites. Creative choices like the fried egg toast with arugula, tomatoes and creme fraiche. Great coffee and nice selection of wines. Nice fresh baked pastries.

VOLTERRA

5411 Ballard Ave, Seattle, 206-789-5100
www.volterrarestaurant.com
CUISINE: Italian
DRINKS: Full bar
SERVING: Mon – Fri dinner only, Sat – Sun breakfast, lunch, and dinner
PRICE RANGE: $$$
NEIGHBORHOOD: Ballard

Chef Don Curtiss offers a Tuscan-inspired menu featuring locally sourced products. Their extensive wine list showcases Italian and Northwest labels. Menu favorites include: Creamy Pesto Pasta with goat cheese and tomatoes and Wild Boar Tenderloin with Gorgonzola Sauce. Great choice for Sunday brunch (breakfast and lunch menus available).

WALRUS AND THE CARPENTER
4743 Ballard Ave NW (bet. 48th St and N 17th Ave), Seattle,
206-395-9227
www.thewalrusbar.com
CUISINE: Seafood, Raw Food, Tapas
DRINKS: Full Bar
SERVING: Dinner from 4 daily
PRICE RANGE: $$$
NEIGHBORHOOD: Ballard
Unprepossessing from its outside (though it's located in
the restored Kolstrand Building), the Walrus is just as
unprepossessing on the inside. Popular seafood eatery with a
beamed ceiling painted white, some seats at the bar and a few
high tops against the wall. Small and cozy. The bottles behind the
bar are displayed in what looks like a big white cupboard, almost
like something you'd find in somebody's house. The oysters of
the day (Malispina, Fanny Bay, Fishhook Fjord, Crystal Rock,
Wolf Beach, etc.) are on view iced down in huge wire baskets
with little chalkboards propped up telling you what variety they
are. You place your order and the shuckers standing there go to
work. They also have the best fried oysters you may ever taste.
Crowds flock here for happy hour because the oysters are priced
really low to bring in the crowds who then buy drinks. A bargain!
Chef Renee Erickson, also of **Boat Street Café**, offers a new
twist on the classic oyster bar. Menu favorites: grilled sardines;

Smoked trout; fried ocean perch. For those who don't want seafood: Steak tartare; Merguez sausages; foie gras. The bar offers a nice selection of wines, craft cocktails and beers.

WESTWARD

2501 N Northlake Way, Seattle, 206-552-8215
www.westwardseattle.com/
CUISINE: American / Mediterranean
DRINKS: Full Bar
SERVING: Dinner nightly; Lunch weekends
PRICE RANGE: $$
NEIGHBORHOOD: Wellingford

This nautical inspired eatery offers Chef Zoi Antonitsas' menu of seafood focused Mediterranean fare. Everything's got a rustic look. Usually has 6 varieties of oysters to choose from. Great things come out of the wood-burning oven: the braised lamb shoulder, or gigante beans with tomato and feta. They have comfortable bar stools at the counter, except that these are the kind that and bolted to the floor so they're hard to move around in. Great views while you sit in an Adirondack chair outside by the fire pit and picnic tables. Boat docking available.

THE WHALE WINS

3506 Stone Way N, Seattle, 206-632-9425
www.thewhalewins.com
CUISINE: American, Small plates
DRINKS: Full bar
SERVING: Lunch, and dinner daily
PRICE RANGE: $$$
NEIGHBORHOOD: Wallingford

This neighborhood restaurant offers a great dining experience including an impressive small plate menu and spirits list. Chef Renee Erickson offers a menu inspired from his favorite places in Europe and England. About her experience here, she says, "The wood oven forces you to cook in a different way. No sautéing!" Menu favorites include: Roasted Whole Trout and Roasted Half Chicken. Delicious selection of desserts like the Rice Pudding with Hazelnut brittle.

WHERE YA AT MATT
Food Truck in downtown Seattle.
www.whereyaatmatt.com
CUISINE: Cajun/Creole/Food Truck
DRINKS: No Booze
SERVING: Lunch, dinner
PRICE RANGE: $
NEIGHBORHOOD: Downtown
Check the website to find the current location of the Creole food truck that serves delicious Po'Boys on New Orleans' style French bread. Po' Boy varieties include: Shrimp, Roast Beef, Creole Pork, Oyster and Smoked Portabella. Also served is jambalaya and gumbo.

WILD GINGER
1401 Third Ave, Seattle, 206-623-4450
www.wildginger.net
CUISINE: Asian Fusion, Thai, Chinese
DRINKS: Full bar
SERVING: Mon – Sat lunch and dinner, Sun dinner only
PRICE RANGE: $$$
NEIGHBORHOOD: Downtown
This eatery offers a unique menu showcasing a variety of Asian cuisine. Menu favorites include: Princess Prawns and Hanoi Tuna. Vegan menu available. Nice creative cocktail menu including after-dinner ports, sherry, and wines. Weekend dim sum brunches.

NIGHTLIFE

BALLARD SMOKE SHOP
5439 Ballard Ave NW (b/t Market St & N 22nd Ave), Seattle,
206-784-6611
www.ballardsmokeshop.com
NEIGHBORHOOD: Ballard
This dive bar (6 am to 11 pm) serves up well whiskey and beer,
in cans and on draft. There's a bell hanging on the wall used
by fishermen who come in after a good catch—they ring it to
indicate the next round is on them. A longtime favorite hangout
even if smoking is no longer allowed. There's also food here,
breakfast (get the salami scramble), to burgers and patty melts,
and even dinner, open-faced hot turkey sandwich. Cheap.

BATHTUB GIN & CO
2205 2nd Ave, Seattle, 206-728-6069
www.bathtubginseattle.com
NEIGHBORHOOD: Belltown
Located in the heart of Belltown, this Speakeasy style bar serves great creative cocktails. All the bartenders are mixologists and really know their shit.

BRAVE HORSE TAVERN
310 Terry Ave N (bet. Thomas St & Harrison St), Seattle, 206-971-0717
www.bravehorsetavern.com
NEIGHBORHOOD: South Lake Union
This friendly tavern is a great place for dinner or late night snack (brick-oven malted pretzels with dipping sauces like beer cheese fondue and smoked peanut butter and bacon) but note that it's a 21 plus venue. Here you'll find a definite tavern atmosphere with a bar that serves over 36 varieties of beer on tap. There are even games like shuffleboard and darts. Weekend and Sunday Brunch is a favorite, with half-priced drinks all day and cornmeal pancakes and smoked brisket hash for breakfast and an excellent fried chicken dinner (from 4:30).

BROUWER'S CAFÉ

400 N 35th St, Seattle, 206-267-2437

www.brouwerscafe.blogspot.com

NEIGHBORHOOD: Freemont

Attracting a lot of Google employees when they get off work, this dive bar has an impressive bar menu with 64 beers on draft (try a couple of the beers made locally—the bartender will help you decide), over 300 bottles, and over 50 Scotches. The kitchen is open until 10 p.m. and the food is good. Happy hour, 3 – 7 p.m., 7 days a week.

CANON

928 12th Ave (bet. Columbia St & Marion St), Seattle, 206-552-9755

www.canonseattle.com

NEIGHBORHOOD: Central District

This popular speakeasy style bar boasts one of the largest spirits collections in the world with 2,800 labels. And they are as serious about their cocktails as any of the characters in "Mad Men." It's not very big so come early to avoid a wait. Dinner is served until 1 a.m. Bartenders here are very adept at making a cocktail to order, so suggest a couple of ingredients and let them show you.

The Back Bar's entrance is located on 2nd & Blanchard

THE CROCODILE

2200 2nd Ave (bet. Bell St & Blanchard St), Seattle 206-441-4618

www.thecrocodile.com

NEIGHBORHOOD: Belltown

This popular music venue has quite an impressive list of the talent that has appeared on their stage including: Beastie Boys, Alabama Shakes, The Melvins, Kulture Shock and Gaslight Anthem. Every music genre has been represented including: hip-hop, rock, electronic, metal, punk, and avant-garde. Cover charge varies depending on band.

KEYS ON MAIN

11 Roy St (bet. N Queen Anne Ave & N 1st Ave), Seattle, 206-270-4444

www.keysonmain.com

NEIGHBORHOOD: Lower Queen Anne

If you're looking for a dueling piano bar then look no farther as this place will play your requests and keep the music rocking all night long. Check the website for show times.

THE KRAKEN BAR & LOUNGE

5257 University Way NE (bet. 52nd St & 55th St), Seattle, 206-522-5334

No web site

NEIGHBORHOOD: University District

This popular dive bar is also a music venue. The music is loud but the drinks are cheap. If you're hungry they have a small menu but the kitchen closes at 8 p.m. Arcade games in the back.

MEDINA HOOKAH LOUNGE

700 S Dearborn St (bet. S 7th Ave & S 8th Ave), Seattle, 206-856-7660

www.medinahookah.com

NEIGHBORHOOD: International District

Known as Seattle's best hookah lounge offering a great variety of shisha flavors. Small membership fee.

NEEDLE AND THREAD
Upstairs at Tavern Law

1406 12th Avenue; 206-325-0133

www.tavernlaw.com

NEIGHBORHOOD: Capitol Hill

This place gets a lot of press because it's, well, a little strange. You go into Tavern Law, a nice little bar, and in the rear there's a phone booth. You go in and the phone dials upstairs. The bartender will tell you to come on up, if there's room, and if there's not, he'll tell you to come back later. (You can reserve, but don't go early or you'll have to wait downstairs at Tavern Law.) Once you get the OK, you go upstairs through an old bank vault and come out in a space tricked out like a speakeasy. Food is the same as downstairs, and it's pretty good. The whole Prohibition theme is fine, but after a while it seems a little too studied for a town like Seattle.

RED DOOR

3401 Evanston Ave, Seattle, 206-547-7521
www.reddoorseattle.com
NEIGHBORHOOD: Freemont
Unpretentious restaurant & neighborhood pub with a simple
menu of sandwiches, burgers, fish and chips, and salads.

ROCK BOX

1603 Nagle Pl, Seattle, 206-302-7625
www.rockboxseattle.com
CUISINE: Karaoke Bar
DRINKS: Beer & Wine Only
SERVING: Dinner; closed Mondays
PRICE RANGE: $$
Japanese-style karaoke club featuring private rooms if you
don't care to sing at the open bar. Always bustling with drunken
singers. Specialty cocktails and snack menu. (The charcuterie
and cheeses come from the nearby restaurant **Cure**, which is
very good.)

THE SHOWBOX

1426 1st Ave, Seattle, 206-628-3151
www.showboxpresents.com
NEIGHBORHOOD: Downtown
This music venue just celebrated its 75th anniversary and
showcases everything from jazz to grunge, and folk to hip hop.
Names that have appeared here include Pearl Jam and burlesque
queen Gypsy Rose Lee. Three bars in the back and tables so you
can watch the concert. Holds over 1,000 people.

TRACTOR TAVERN

5213 Ballard Ave NW (bet. N 20th Ave & Vernon Pl), Seattle,
206-789-3599

www.tractortavern.com

NEIGHBORHOOD: Ballard

This casual music venue showcases primarily country bands. The
good thing is that you can hail a cab in this upscale neighborhood
without any fear. The place has a divey atmosphere but it's not
as dirty as it looks. Always has an interesting line-up of bands.
(They even have square dancing on Mondays.) Check website for
schedule. Cover changes depending on band.

THE TRIPLE DOOR

216 Union St, Seattle, 206-838-4333

www.thetripledoor.net

NEIGHBORHOOD: Downtown

This downtown theatre has been reimagined as great restaurant
and music venue that offers world-class entertainment and
award-winning cuisine from **Wild Ginger** next door. Menu
favorites include: Panang Beef Curry and Wild Ginger Fragrant
Duck. In the mainstage theatre you'll find national and
international touring acts while the lounge features an eclectic
variety of live music. No cover.

THE UPSTAIRS

2209 2nd Ave (bet. Bell St & Blanchard St), Seattle, 206-441-4013

www.theupstairsseattle.com

NEIGHBORHOOD: Belltown

This neighborhood bar is small so get used to the crowded scene. Bar offers a nice list of creative cocktails and beers. Happy Hour: 5 – 8 p.m. One bartender so there's often a wait for drinks.

THE VERA PROJECT

Seattle Center

305 Harrison St, Seattle, 206-956-8372

www.theveraproject.org

NEIGHBORHOOD: Lower Queen Anne

This is an all-ages volunteer music and arts venue with a focus on ages 14 – 24. The Vera Project offers a variety of events including concerts, art exhibits, and classes.

INDEX

Other Books by the Same Author

Andrew Delaplaine has written in widely varied fields: screenplays, novels (adult and juvenile), travel writing, journalism. His books are available in quality bookstores as well as all online retailers.

JACK HOUSTON / ST. CLAIR POLITICAL THRILLERS

THE KEYSTONE FILE – PART 1
THE KEYSTONE FILE – PART 2
THE KEYSTONE FILE – PART 3
THE KEYSTONE FILE – PART 4
THE KEYSTONE FILE – PART 5
THE KEYSTONE FILE – PART 6
THE KEYSTONE FILE – PART 7 *(FINAL)*

On Election night, as China and Russia mass soldiers on their common border in preparation for war, there's a tie in the Electoral College that forces the decision for President into the House of Representatives as mandated by the Constitution. The incumbent Republican President, working through his Aide for Congressional Liaison, uses the Keystone File, which contains dirt on every member of Congress, to blackmail members into supporting the Republican candidate. The action runs from Election Night in November to Inauguration Day on January 20. Jack Houston St. Clair runs a small detective agency in Miami. His father is Florida Governor Sam Houston St. Clair, the Republican candidate. While he tries to help his dad win the election, Jack also gets hired to follow up on some suspicious wire transfers involving drug smugglers, leading him to a sunken narco-sub off Key West that has $65 million in cash in its hull.

THE RUNNING MATE

Sam Houston St. Clair has been President for four long years and right now he's bogged down in a nasty fight to be re-elected. A Secret Service agent protecting the opposing candidate discovers that the candidate is sleeping with someone he shouldn't be, and tells his lifelong friend, the President's son Jack, this vital information so Jack can pass it on to help his father win the election. The candidate's wife has also found out about the clandestine affair and plots to kill the lover if her husband wins the election. Jack goes to Washington, and becomes involved in an international whirlpool of intrigue.

AFTER THE OATH: DAY ONE
AFTER THE OATH: MARCH WINDS
WEDDING AT THE WHITE HOUSE

Only three months have passed since Sam Houston St. Clair was sworn in as the new President, but a lot has happened. Returning from Vienna where he met with Russian and Chinese diplomats, Sam is making his way back to Flagler Hall in Miami, his first trip home since being inaugurated. Son Jack is in the midst of turmoil of his own back in Miami, dealing with various dramas, not the least of which is his increasing alienation from Babylon Fuentes and his growing attraction to the seductive Lupe Rodriguez. Fernando Pozo addresses new problems as he struggles to expand Cuba's secret operations in the U.S., made even more difficult as U.S.-Cuban relations thaw. As his father returns home, Jack knows Sam will find as much trouble at home as he did in Vienna.

THE ADVENTURES OF SHERLOCK HOLMES IV

In this series, the original Sherlock Holmes's great-great-great grandson solves crimes and mysteries in the present day, working out of the boutique hotel he owns on South Beach.

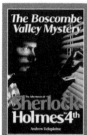
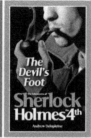

THE BOSCOMBE VALLEY MYSTERY

Sherlock Holmes and Watson are called to a remote area of Florida overlooking Lake Okeechobee to investigate a murder where all the evidence points to the victim's son as the killer. Holmes, however, is not so sure.

THE DEVIL'S FOOT

Holmes's doctor orders him to take a short holiday in Key West, and while there, Holmes is called on to look into a case in which three people involved in a Santería ritual died with no explanation.

THE CLEVER ONE

A former nun who, while still very devout, has renounced her vows so that she could "find a life, and possibly love, in the real world." She comes to Holmes in hopes that he can find out what happened to the man who promised to marry her, but mysteriously disappeared moments before their wedding.

THE COPPER BEECHES

A nanny reaches out to Sherlock Holmes seeking his advice on whether she should take a new position when her prospective employer has demanded that she cut her hair as part of the job.

THE RED-HAIRED MAN

A man with a shock of red hair calls on Sherlock Holmes to solve the mystery of the Red-haired League.

THE SIX NAPOLEONS

Inspector Lestrade calls on Holmes to help him figure out why a madman would go around Miami breaking into homes and businesses to destroy cheap busts of the French Emperor. It all seems very insignificant to Holmes—until, of course, a murder occurs.

THE MAN WITH THE TWISTED LIP

In what seems to be the case of a missing person, Sherlock Holmes navigates his way through a maze of perplexing clues that leads him through a sinister world to a surprising conclusion.

THE BORNHOLM DIAMOND

A mysterious Swedish nobleman requests a meeting to discuss a matter of such serious importance that it may threaten the line of succession in one of the oldest royal houses in Europe.

SEVERAL TITLES IN THE DELAPLAINE SERIES OF PRE-SCHOOL READERS FOR CHILDREN

THE DELAPLAINE LONG WEEKEND TRAVEL GUIDE SERIES

Delaplaine Travel Guides represent the author's take on some of the many cities he's visited and many of which he has called home (for months or even years) during a lifetime of travel. The books are available as either ebooks or as printed books. Owing to the ease with which material can be uploaded, both the printed and ebook editions are updated 3 times a year.

Atlanta	Memphis
Austin	Mérida (Mexico)
Boston	Mexico City
Cancún (Mexico)	Miami & South Beach
Cannes	Milwaukee
Cape Cod	Myrtle Beach
Charleston	Nantucket
Chicago	Napa Valley
Clearwater – St. Petersburg	Naples & Marco Island
Fort Lauderdale	Nashville
Fort Myers & Sanibel	New Orleans
Gettysburg	Newport (R.I.)
Hamptons, The	Philadelphia
Hilton Head	Portland (Ore.)
Key West & the Florida Keys	Provincetown
Las Vegas	San Juan
Lima (Peru)	Sarasota
Louisville	Savannah
Marseille	Seattle
Martha's Vineyard	Tampa Bay

THE FOOD ENTHUSIAST'S COMPLETE RESTAURANT GUIDES

9 781640 227880